MW00451217

Violin Elementary Progressive Studies Set I

*Twenty-four studies
in the first position*

Herbert Kinsey

ABRSM

Published by ABRSM (Publishing) Ltd, a wholly owned subsidiary of ABRSM
Printed in England by Caligraving Ltd, Thetford, Norfolk,
on materials from sustainable sources
Reprinted in 2019

TWENTY-FOUR
ELEMENTARY PROGRESSIVE STUDIES

FIRST POSITION

HERBERT KINSEY

1

1st, 2nd and 3rd Fingers
Semitones between 1st and 2nd Fingers

2

1st, 2nd and 3rd Fingers
Semitones between 2nd and 3rd Fingers

WHOLE BOWS

A. B. 432

3

1st, 2nd and 3rd Fingers
Exercise for Legato Crossing of Strings

4

1st, 2nd and 3rd Fingers
Exercise for Strengthening the Fingers

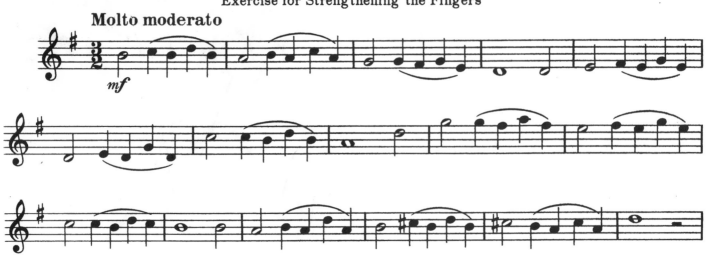

5

1st, 2nd and 3rd Fingers

Scale Passages. Firm Bowing

Alla marcia

6

1st, 2nd and 3rd Fingers
Legato Playing

Andante sostenuto

7

1st, 2nd and 3rd Fingers
Scale Passages

Andantino

8

1st, 2nd and 3rd Fingers, with occasional use of 4th Finger

9

1st, 2nd and 3rd Fingers
Exercise for Strengthening the Fingers

10

All the Fingers
Exercise for Lifting the Bow *

* Should be played near the heel. Use about one third of the bow.

11

Preparatory Exercise for Trills

12

Arpeggio Exercise

13

Varied Bowings

14

Preparatory Exercise for Trills

15

Varied Bowings

16

Preparatory Exercise for Trills

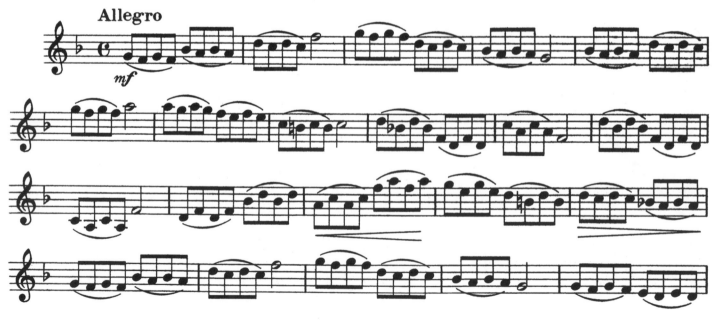

17

Exercise for developing the independence of the Fingers

Legato Bowing

Allegretto

18
Lifted Bowing near the Heel

19

Preparatory Exercise for Trills, with Scale Passages

Allegro risoluto

20
Spiccato Bowing

21

Exercise for the smooth joining of the Bows

22

Scale Passages and Spiccato Bowing

23

Varied Bowings

24

Varied Bowings